Rocky Mountain
WILDFLOWERS

Text and Photos by Kent & Donna Dannen

Tundra Publications
1997 Big Owl Road
Allenspark, Colorado 80510

Copyright 1981 by Kent & Donna Dannen

Library of Congress Cataloging in Publication Data

Dannen, Kent 1946-
   Rocky Mountain wildflowers.

   Includes index.
   1. Wild flowers--Rocky Mountains--Identification.
I. Dannen, Donna, 1949-   II. Title.
QK139.D36   582.13'0978   81-7439
                                                          AACR2

ISBN 0-9606768-0-5

This book is dedicated to our fellow faculty members of the National Wildlife Federation's Conservation Summit, who have informed and inspired our attitudes toward the earth and the plants which clothe it. Specific knowledge about Rocky Mountain wildflowers has been shared generously by the following Summit experts who are responsible for much that is good in this book.

E.H. Brunquist
Mary Jane Foley
Bruno Klinger
Dodie and Stan Mulaik
Ruth Ashton Nelson
Joyce Ann Powers
Leila and John Shultz
Deborah Steward
Robert K. Webb
Beatrice Willard

CONTENTS

	PAGE
TRY A WILD ALTERNATIVE	5
"THE FLOWERS APPEAR ON THE EARTH..."	6
BLUE FLOWERS	9
YELLOW FLOWERS	20
RED FLOWERS	33
WHITE FLOWERS	49
INDEX	64

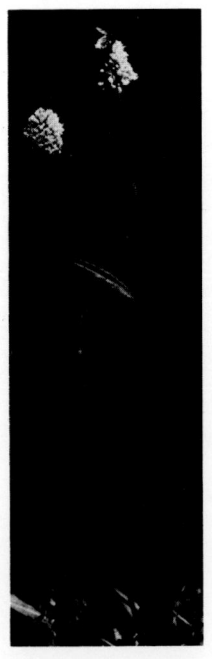

AMERICAN BISTORT, *Polygonum bistortoides,* is one of the most common flowers bobbing in alpine and subalpine meadows. Its twisted, horizontal rootstalk has given this plant the name of snakeweed and has been used for food around the world, by bears as well as by people. The red stem with knobs at intervals resembles a fishing pole and accounts for another name, knotweed. Buckwheat Family, 3/10 life size.

TRY A WILD ALTERNATIVE

We assume that anything wild gets along fine without human interference. But to enjoy wildflowers often and conveniently around home and workplace, we need to plant seeds or plants. Once established, wildflowers do tend to flourish with little care, a beautiful alternative to high-maintenance lawns and gardens.

Salvaging wild plants from construction sites is satisfying but also haphazard and time-consuming. Collecting plants that otherwise would be destroyed is the only acceptable reason to try to move wildflowers that already are benefitting the spot where they happen to be growing. Even collecting wildflower seeds may reduce the number of flowers that will grow in that area in the future.

Using commercially produced wildflower seeds is the most effective way to establish wildflowers around areas of human development. But seeds need to be planted with care and planning to have a good chance of growing. Buy seed mixes that contain only species adapted to the climate in which they are to be planted.

Planting in fall mimics natural seed distribution. Some seeds need winter cold to germinate, though refrigeration can shortcut this requirement. Planted in spring or summer, perennial flowers may not bloom for a year or two. Besides perennials, most commercial seed mixes also contain annuals which bloom faster, providing color until the perennials get going for the long haul.

Ideally, the seeds should be planted on bare ground without competition from other plants. Rough up the soil a bit with a rake, broadcast the seeds, then press them into contact with the soil.

Inadequate watering during the first three weeks after planting is a major obstacle to successful wildflower propagation in the Rockies, where moisture usually is unreliable. Often, where you want wildflowers is inconvenient to irrigate. Nonetheless, a deep watering right after planting followed by frequent light waterings will significantly boost your success rate. Other initial problems include wind, hard rain, blowing seeds of undesirable plants, and hungry birds and small mammals.

Reducing these problems are seeds from Applewood Seed Company, a nationally known supplier of wildflower seed since 1965. Applewood tests their seeds in the laboratory and field, and the company has been a leader in wildflower research for many years. Their mail order flyer lists more than 50 species and 15 wildflower mixtures to meet many different growing requirements. Ordering information is available on the internet at applewoodseed.com, or by writing Applewood Seed Company, 5310 Vivian Street, Arvada CO 80002.

"THE FLOWERS APPEAR ON THE EARTH..."

The intrepid adventurer who creeps up to capture red elephants and yellow monkeys in the Rocky Mountains is not hallucinating. These colorful species are among the thousands pursued in one of the most joyful, creative, and beautiful types of outdoor recreation—wildflower photography.

Little red elephants and yellow monkeyflowers inhabit wet sites in the mostly arid Rockies. But each habitat type—dry, sunny, shaded, deep soil rich in some kinds of minerals, sand holding traces of other minerals—has its typical flower species. Over five thousand species growing over the whole blooming Rockies guarantee that photographers never run out of new subjects.

Everyone likes wildflower photos—in reasonable numbers. "Reasonable" is defined by the skill of the photographer. Skill is of two types. Technical skill can be mastered by anyone with a few hundred dollars to spend on equipment and the physical ability to tolerate some discomfort. Artistic skill interprets the texture, form, and color of flowers on film. Knowledge about flowers helps increase artistic skill, primarily by increasing variety among flower photographs.

Anyone can take a satisfying flower photo with any type of camera. However, the number of satisfying flower photos you can capture is severely limited if you are not using a single lens reflex (SLR) camera capable of moving in very close to flowers. Special close-up equipment includes supplementary lenses, extension tubes, bellows, and a macro lens. One or more of these items is a necessity for flower photography. At various times, telephoto and wide angle lenses also are useful.

Flower photography discomfort comes because photographers and flowers are built on different scales. Photographers usually have to reduce their statures to flower height. This means contorting the body into various uncomfortable positions for agonizing lengths of time to get the eye behind the camera's viewfinder at ground level. And even the most limber acrobat or a photographer with a right angle viewfinder cannot avoid the rocks, thorns, and biting bugs.

It can be dangerous. Donna has had to climb down a cliff via a poison ivy vine to position herself for an orchid photo. Far worse, a sharp, grass-like sedge once pierced her eye as she moved in on the adjacent alpine wallflower. Kent had to avoid an explosive booby trap set to maim anyone who tried to dig up a somewhat valuable wild ginseng flower he was photographing in the Appalachian Mountains.

Artistic photos of wildflowers may involve several elements. Most people think of color first when they consider wildflower beauty. Thus, this book is organized by color.

But the form of blossoms and leaves is another element in their beauty. Texture—hairy, bumpy, or smooth surfaces of leaves, stems, or flowers—is a third aspect that can be exploited to create lovely pictures. Some of the best photos in this book are black and white, emphasizing form and texture.

SALSIFY seed head, life size (see page 31)

Photo purpose also figures importantly in artistic composition. Is the picture's only purpose to be an impression of form, texture, or color? Or is it intended for identification, frequently showing leaves or other important plant parts? Whatever the purpose of the picture, photographers receive considerable comfort in knowing that, while some flower photos are better than others, it is nearly impossible to make an ugly flower photo.

Indeed, flowers long have symbolized perfect beauty. Green leaves and stems do yeoman work for plants and all living things, creating food from the minerals of the earth in chlorophyll factories powered by the sun. But very pleasant, peaceful, hard-working green is a trifle dull. Flowers give us explosions of exciting colors and shapes on a prosaic field of green.

As reproductive organs, flowers are nature's extravagances. Plants can reproduce well without flowers, as is indicated by many tons of coal formed of non-flowering plants some 345 million years ago. Not until 130 million years ago did flowering plants bloom as examples of nature's inherent impulse to emphasize beauty beyond strict necessity.

Some folks deny such foolishness, maintaining that humans imagine beauty. Flowers exist to attract insects to efficiently pollinate seeds, making them fertile. We merely learn to regard flowers as beautiful.

But, while it is true that flowers exist to produce seeds, it is equally true that seeds exist to produce flowers. If nature produced humans concerned about beauty after survival was assured, why could not the rest of nature contain a similar impulse to produce beauty beyond the needs of reproduction?

Another similarity between flowers and people impressed ancient observers of nature who penned the Bible. The bulk of biblical references to wildflowers use them as analogies to brevity of human life. Well-known exceptions from the Song of Solomon (such as,". . .the winter is past, the rain is over and gone; the flowers appear on the earth. . .") celebrate human erotic love, a beauty as fleeting in its way as wild blooms are.

The typical biblical view of wildflowers is tinged with melancholy that we feel when enjoying them today. Psalm 103:15 could have been composed during a spring chinook wind in the Rockies:

> *As for man, his days are as grass; as a flower of the field, so he flourisheth. For the wind passeth over it, and it is gone, and the place thereof shall know it no more.*

The Rockies offset brief blooming of individual wildflowers by extending the blooming season through various altitudes. Explosions of color begin in the foothills and a month later have advanced up the mountains to the montane zone of open, sunny woods. In mid summer, the blooming season skips over the dense, snow-filled subalpine forest to carpet mountaintop tundra with glory that takes away whatever breath you have left at 11,000 to 14,000 feet above sea level. When the snow finally melts below treeline, subalpine forests produce the most luxurient flower display of all.

Wildflower photography can do much to emphasize the joy and gratitude evoked by such blooming extravaganzas. The joy comes not so much from partially preserving these floral glories on film, although the reminders are nice to have. Much more important than the photos themselves is the act of taking them.

While going through the contortions and effort of picturing wildflowers, you are communing with them. When the pictures have been taken, you know that you have experienced the flowers as thoroughly as possible. You have not wasted the wonder. And, no matter what the quality of the pictures on the film, the quality of the pictures on your soul will enrich your life forever.

BLUE FLOWERS

COLORADO BLUE COLUMBINE, *Aquilegia caerulea,* Buttercup Family, ⅓ life size.

COLORADO BLUE COLUMBINE has spurs, as befits the official floral symbol of a western state. But, when pioneer botanist Edwin James discovered this remarkable beauty in 1820, its spurs at once identified it as cousin to species already known from eastern America, Europe, and Asia.

Columbine spurs protrude from the flower as reservoirs for nectar. Insects or hummingbirds that feed from these deep reservoirs brush against many stamens laden with yellow pollen. The nectar-feeder then transfers the pollen on its body to the next columbine it visits, stimulating fertilization of seeds. Sometimes, however, an insect bores into a columbine spur's tip, stealing the nectar without performing any fertilization service.

Nonetheless, the spurs encouraged enough fertilization so that blue columbine once were abundant from shady aspen groves at 6,000 feet to alpine boulder fields at 12,000 feet. In 1899, Colorado blue columbine was decreed by law to be the state flower. But public love led to misguided columbine picking and digging, destroying the abundance which modern admirers only can imagine.

Conservation efforts by the Colorado Mountain Club were followed by the first state law protecting columbine in 1925. Growing public awareness that wildflowers should be left where they grow has been offset somewhat by increased public use of columbine habitat. Thus, while the percentage of enlightened folks in the wilds has increased, so has the actual number of unenlightened flower pickers, who are attracted to showy columbine.

Colorado's Recreation Land Preservation Act of 1971 makes it illegal on public land "To willfully cut down, break, or otherwise destroy any living tree, shrubbery, wild flowers, or natural flora..." Maximum fine is $500.

The spurs, as the columbine's most obvious feature, gave the flower its scientific name. But just what *Aquilegia* means is disputed. Some experts credit the spurs' resemblance to eagle talons and point to the Latin word *aquila,* which means eagle. Others maintain that *Aquilegia* comes from the Latin words *aqua* (water) and *legere* (to collect), referring to the nectar in the spurs. Further complicating the confusion is a fancied resemblance of some columbine species to a dove *(columba* in Latin), from which the popular name comes. At least it is certain that *caerulea* means blue.

Nine columbine species are found in the Rockies. See Rocky Mountain red columbine on page 44.

DWARF BLUE COLUMBINE,
Aquilegia saximontana, Buttercup Family, life size.

DWARF BLUE COLUMBINE or Rocky Mountain columbine (*saximontana* means Rocky Mountain) blooms among protecting boulders above treeline in July. It is just as lovely as the state flower and much rarer, hence, more exciting to find. Dwarf columbine's stubby, hooked spurs and small size are attributed to its harsh alpine environment. But large Colorado blues bobbing in the breeze among nearby boulders imply a more complex reason than simple miniaturization through tribulation.

Ironically, Colorado blue columbine grows widely throughout the Rockies (although most colorfully in Colorado), while little Rocky Mountain columbine is native only to Colorado. Except for the fact that only high country hikers and climbers ever see the dwarf columbine, it might make a more appropriate state flower.

TANSY-ASTER is the most conspicuous purple composite in the late summer and fall. It thrives on disturbed soil and is seen frequently by humans, who, along the with pocket gophers, are great soil disturbers. Tansy-aster is not technically an aster, which is why its name is hyphenated. With hyphens botanists cross their fingers behind their backs, implying, "We don't really mean it." True asters are distinguished from tansy-asters by the recurving tips of tansy-aster bracts, the leaves enclosing the base of the flower head. *Aster bigelovii* commemorates exploring botanist John Bigelow (see dark penstemon, page 12).

For mere mortals, distinguishing tansy-asters from true asters of various species is not as important as separating asters from daisies. Asters have broader and fewer rays, the petal-like rim flowers on composite flowers, making them somewhat neater than scruffy daisies. Daisies tend to bloom in early summer, while asters tend to be the purple composites of fall.

ASPEN DAISY is the commonest of its family in the montane zone. It favors wet aspen groves and meadows and forest edges. Usually it bears several flowers on a nonhairy stem clasped by smooth leaves. *Speciosus* means pretty, and this flower also is called showy daisy. Very similar dryland daisy (*Erigeron subtrinervis*) grows in dry areas near aspen daisy and has a hairy stem with buds that tend to droop.

The literal translation of the Greek words forming *Erigeron* is "early old man." This ambiguous title may refer to woolly seedheads in the spring. Or it may be best translated "soon becoming old," indicating that the many narrow rays wilt almost at once after the flower is picked.

TANSY-ASTER, *Aster bigelovii*, Composite Family, life size.

ASPEN DAISY, *Erigeron speciosus*, Composite Family, ½ life size.

TALL ONE-SIDE PENSTEMON, *Penstemon unilateralis,* Figwort Family, ¼ life size.

TALL ONE-SIDE PENSTEMON is one of the most abundant of the 250 penstemon species native to North America. Penstemon means five stamens, although only four of these pollen producers grow in the tubular flowers. The fifth stamen is infertile and is called a staminode. Frequently, the staminode is elongated and covered with hairs. This trait gave penstemons their common name, beard tongue.

Usually over a foot high, tall one-side penstemon flourishes on overgrazed pastures and areas of disturbed soil, such as roadsides. Its staminode usually is not hairy. From this common plant, Indians brewed a wide variety of medicinal concoctions, supposedly good for most conceivable ills. *Unilateralis* means one side, pointing out the pattern of flower arrangement on the stem.

LOW PENSTEMON grows thickly among rocks. Its dark blue flowers are hairy and perhaps a bit sticky. In some years, the blooms of penstemon are so abundant that they turn the foothills a misty blue in May and June. From this spectacle comes the alternate name, blue mist penstemon. In the montane and subalpine zones later in summer, low penstemon is common, but masses of blue more likely are tall one-side penstemon. *Virens* means green and refers to the particularly shiny, green leaves.

DARK PENSTEMON, a common resident of the well-watered subalpine zone, is typically hairy. One variety is a dingy white, often growing beside very dark specimens. The species was discovered in New Mexico's Sandia Mountains by Dr. John Bigelow, an army surgeon who served as botanist on an 1853 exporation to find railroad routes. This survey by the Topographical Engineers was led by Captain Amiel Weeks Whipple, hence dark penstemon's scientific name, *whippleanus.*

LOW PENSTEMON, *Penstemon virens,* Figwort Family, ¼ life size.

DARK PENSTEMON, *Penstemon whippleanus,* Figwort Family, 3/5 life size.

SILVERY LUPINE resembles the Texas bluebonnet and spreads its five-finger leaflets among sagebrush bushes and lodgepole pines. Hybrids among lupines are common. Frozen lupine seeds recovered from a lemming burrow in 1967 were estimated to be 10,000 years old. They germinated two days after they were planted. Lupine seeds are thrown from mature pods with considerable strength, emerging with a soft pop. Since most lupines are poisonous to a degree, they should not be eaten under any circumstances. *Argenteus* means silvery.

SILVERY LUPINE, *Lupinus argenteus,* Pea Family, ¼ life size.

AMERICAN PASQUEFLOWER, *Anemone patens (Pulsatilla hirsuitissima),* Buttercup Family, ½ life size.

AMERICAN PASQUEFLOWER is named for the Pasqual or Easter season, when the plant supposedly blooms. Actually, this announcer of spring's resurrection may show its lavender blossom as early as March on the prairies and spring up after the snow melts at treeline in July. Few flowers are more eagerly looked for by winter-weary westerners. Pasqueflower stems continue to grow after the blooming period. When clusters of silky plumes indicate that fertile seeds are about to float away on the wind, they are several inches higher than were the flowers.

WESTERN BLUE FLAG, *Iris missouriensis,* Iris Family, ½ life size.

WESTERN BLUE FLAG is similar to garden irises and easily recognized. Dependent on a moist environment, wild iris can turn fields blue after a wet spring. This is particularly true if the fields are heavily grazed by livestock. With an acrid taste, beautiful blue flag is little liked for grazing. It thrives while competing grasses are eaten. Its bad taste is fortunate for the animals as well as for the iris, which is toxic. Indians made a reputedly deadly arrow poison from it.

Despite being called *missouriensis,* western blue flag does not grow in Missouri. It was named by pioneering botanist Thomas Nuttall for the Missouri River, along which he found his first specimens in the early 1830's in Montana or the Dakotas.

MONKSHOOD is an aptly named flower of which approximately 300 species are listed in Eurasia and North America. The only species in the Rockies is *columbianum,* named for the Columbia River. Most monkshood flowers are purple, but a white variety is found occassionally in the Rockies.

Very attractive and very poisonous, this helmet-shaped flower is closely related to larkspur. The poison, aconite, which monkshood contains once was used medicinally to reduce fever and is used today as a heart sedative. This drug is obtained principally from a European species, *Aconitum nappellus.* The same species is celebrated as wolfbane; no one who has hung a sprig of monkshood around his or her neck ever has been attacked by a werewolf.

MONKSHOOD, *Aconitum columbianum,* Buttercup Family, ½ life size.

SUBALPINE LARKSPUR is a delphinium, a group that includes 250 species of wild and domestic flowers. About two dozen species grow wild in the Rockies, varying from short Nelson larkspur to mountain larkspur, growing between three and seven feet tall in montane zone aspen groves. Closely related to monkshood, some species of larkspur resemble their helmet-shaped cousin from a distance. But close inspection shows that a protruding spur easily indentifies delphiniums.

Larkspur and monkshood both are just as poisonous as they are attractive. Larkspur seems to be the more dangerous of the two for cattle. Elk avoid eating some larkspurs in spring but consume it with gusto in late summer and fall. Perhaps larkspur loses its toxin after blooming. Indians who called delphinium sleeproot dusted it in gambling opponents' food to make them drowsy. A little more might have wiped out the need to pay off any loses.

SUBALPINE LARKSPUR,
Delphinium barbeyi,
Buttercup Family, ½ life size.

ALPINE FORGET-ME-NOTS, *Eritrichium aretioides,* Borage Family, life size. Yellow flowers are drabas.

ALPINE FORGET-ME-NOTS, among the first blooms on the tundra, almost vibrate with the intensity of their blue color. Their deep blue indicates the presence of much anthocyanin, a pigment that converts light to heat. Forget-me-nots need all available heat to survive subfreezing alpine spring, which never remembers that winter is supposed to be past. Some forget-me-nots are white, but blues are far more common, perhaps due to extra warmth from their anthocyanin. Both whites and blues are hairy ground-huggers in order to defeat cold and dehydration on the windy tundra. *Eritrichium* comes from the Greek words for wool and hair.

GREENLEAF CHIMINGBELLS, *Mertensia viridis,* Borage Family, ½ life size.

GREENLEAF CHIMINGBELLS or mertensia or bluebells represent a wide-ranging clan of approximately fifty species in Eurasia and North America. Botanists identify 35 species in the Rockies alone; hybrids are common. Mere mortals identify two kinds: tall and short. Tall chimingbells *(Mertensia ciliata)* are particularly conspicuous, standing three feet tall along subalpine streams. Wildlife from elk to pica favor this mertensia for forage. Greenleaf chimingbells tend to have greener leaves than the bluegreen leaves of tall chimingbells. But the chief difference is the six-inch height of the greenleaf, which grows on the alpine tundra. Languid lady is another charming name applied to all the popular mertensia.

PURPLE FRINGE,
Phacelia sericia,
Waterleaf Family.
¾ life size.

SKY PILOT,
Polemonium viscosum,
Phlox Family.
½ life size.

PURPLE FRINGE grows in sandy, rocky soil, particularly in disturbed soil along roads. Several stems form clusters of dark purple stalks that look fringed from a distance. Up close, though, you can see that each "fringe" is a delicate stamen tipped with orange-yellow pollen. Almost fern-like leaves are covered with silky hairs. These throw a silver tone into the green leaves and stem and give purple fringe its scientific name: *sericea* means silky.

SKY PILOT also favors disturbed soils along roads or soil excavated by a natural earthmover — the pocket gopher. Together with bright yellow alpine sunflower and alpine wallflower, sky pilot and purple fringe are the showiest blooms in tundra color explosions called "gopher gardens" in honor of the critter that gets them going.

Unlike purple fringe, sky pilot is restricted to the alpine tundra. Its orange pollen stands out boldly against the blue of its trumpet-shaped flowers, an attractive color pattern for pollinating insects. Named for its high altitude home and color, sky pilot is called just as correctly, if not as poetically, skunkweed. If smelled from a few inches away or if stepped on, sky pilot inflicts a memorable stench. The odor comes from sticky hairs that cover the leaves and stem. *Viscosum* means sticky. Frequently growing adjacent to sky pilot is honey polemonium *(Polemonium brandegei),* a cream-colored version of sky pilot.

SUBALPINE JACOB'S LADDER,
Polemonium delicatum,
Phlox Family,
⅓ life size.

SUBALPINE JACOB'S LADDER, because it is somewhat smaller than the version familiar to wanderers in eastern woods, is called *delicatum*. The paired leaflets, like rungs along the leaf's midrib, climb toward heavenly blue blossoms. The name comes from the biblical patriarch Jacob, who was walking in the wilds when night came. Deciding to camp, Jacob lay down in a rocky place with a stone for a pillow. In this not-very-comfortable sleep, he had a dream in which God stood at the top of a ladder extending from earth to heaven. God promised Jacob that his many descendants would cover the earth (Genesis 28:11-14). This must be why there are so many hikers and campers today.

MOUNTAIN HAREBELL,
Campanula rotundifolia,
Bellflower Family, ¾ life size.

MOUNTAIN HAREBELL is in the running to be the most common wildflower in the Rockies. It grows from the foothills to treeline, where it is replaced by the very similar alpine harebell *(Campanula uniflora).* Close relatives (such as the Scottish bluebell) are well-known in Eurasia, where harebell was named. Also called witches' thimble, this charming flower seems to have fallen into bad associations, for witches were deemed able to turn themselves into hares. It was bad luck to have a hare/witch cross your path.

The scientific name makes equally dubious sense. *Campanula* means little bell, which accurately describes the flower drooping to protect its pollen in the rain. But *rotundifolia* means round leaf, while mountain harebell leaves tend to be heart-shaped or grass-like. Harebell spreads rapidly along underground stems, leading fussy gardeners to apply unrepeatable names to this hardy volunteer.

LEWIS FLAX is named for Meriwether Lewis of the Lewis and Clark expedition. Indians made twine with flax, and its relatives have been used for thousands of years to make fiber. *Linum* gave us the fabric and word linen. Linseed oil is extracted from flax as are medicines and pigments. But not the least of its values is the beauty bestowed by Lewis flax flowers, opening one per day in the morning, withering in the hot sun, dropping its delicate petals, and adding another seedpod to the row lining the stalk.

LEWIS FLAX, *Linum lewisii*, Flax Family, ¾ life size.

SUBALPINE BLUE VIOLET is the commonest of its beloved family in the Rockies. It favors streambanks, shady woods, and moist tundra slopes, blooming as spring climbs from the montane zone to treeline in June, July, and August. *Adunca* means hooked.

DWARF BLUEBERRY forms green mats in lodgepole pine forests in the subalpine zone. The juicy berries that follow these urn-shaped flowers are certain to delay the journey of passing hikers. Wildlife also devours dwarf blueberry and its cousins, leaves and twigs and all. Bears, in particular, crave blueberries. But ursine digestive systems process flesh better than fruit, and bear scats during berry season often are dotted by undigested blueberries.

SUBALPINE BLUE VIOLET, *Viola adunca*, Violet Family and **DWARF BLUEBERRY**, *Vaccinium caespitosum*, Heath Family, life size.

ALPINE WALLFLOWER, *Erysimum nivale,* Mustard Family, plus sky pilot, alpine avens, American bistort, and alpine sunflower.

YELLOW FLOWERS

ALPINE WALLFLOWER seems too conspicuously pretty to bear such a prosaic name. It may have the lovliest fragrance of any flower in the Rockies. The wallflower clan was named for one species' tendency to grow near walls. Lasses who remained near ballroom walls, unasked to dance, were named for the flower. Alpine wallflower blooms early on the tundra, and its stem continues to elongate after blooming is done. *Nivale* means "of snow."

Western Wallflower *(Erysimum asperum)* grows on tall stems below treeline, blanketing montane meadows with yellow after wet springs. Also called blister cress, the *Erysimum* clan takes its name from the Greek word meaning to draw blisters. Pungent wallflower juice has been used for that purpose.

Wallflowers are mustards, as indicated by their four petals in a cross arrangement. Indians used mustard seeds to flavor foods. Many important domestic vegetables and many bothersome weeds also belong to the mustard family.

BUTTER-AND-EGGS is an alien flower, brought from Europe to American gardens, from which it escaped. It is most common in disturbed soils—roadsides, trail margins, mine dumps. Butter-and-eggs spreads aggressively by its creeping roots. The inch-long spur contains nectar, guaranteeing that most feeding insects or hummingbirds will have to penetrate the bloom far enough to pick up pollen and to leave some from the previous butter-and-eggs they visited. Butter-and-eggs also is called toadflax because the mouth of the nectary looks like a toad's mouth, and the leaves resemble flax foliage.

BUTTER-AND-EGGS,
Linaria vulgaris,
Figwort Family, ¾ life size.

PLAINS PRICKLY PEAR CACTUS also is called starvation cactus. For a plant whose scientific name, *polyacantha,* means many-spined, plains prickly pear is surprisingly edible. The big spines are obvious and can be removed in various ways. But a second tier of hook-shaped thorns are so small as to be seen best with a magnifying lens. An archeologist examining feces of cliff dwellers at Mesa Verde National Park found many small prickly pear spines that had been eaten centuries ago (so much for the romance of archeology). When used as an emergency cattle food after the spines have been burned off, prickly pear may indicate that the emergency was caused by too many cattle overgrazing the land. The spiny pads may break off and stick on noses of beleaguered cattle.

PLAINS PRICKLY PEAR CACTUS,
Opuntia polyacantha,
Cactus Family, ½ life size.

SNOW LILY or **GLACIER LILY,**
Erythronium grandiflorum,
Lily Family, ⅙ life size.

SNOW LILY or **GLACIER LILY** is a lovely follower of melting snowbanks in the subalpine zone to treeline. Sometimes the distinctive pair of smooth shiny leaves push their way up before the snow has melted, flanking one to three delicate yellow buds. Soon the buds blossom in the brilliant splendor indicated by their scientific name, *grandiflorum,* which seems more appropriately elegant than its literal translation, big-flowered. After the flowering is done, the leaves turn a yellow-tan that continues to color marshy areas well into late summer. Although Indians ate glacier lilies frequently, modern wilderness travelers are too entranced by the flowers' beauty to dine on them. Bears are less fussy and relish digging out the bulbs to devour. Close relatives of this lily inhabit eastern American woods and Eurasia.

YELLOW STONECROP is a sedum, one of the large family of dryness-tolerant flowers domesticated for home and garden. A waxy covering on the succulent leaves helps prevent water loss. The very common yellow stonecrop covers rocky ground from the plains to peak tops. Its reddish-green rosettes of leaves come up early, but the yellow cluster of star-shaped flowers blossom later. Botanists distinguish various species of yellow stonecrop, such as *lanceolatum* (lance-leafed) and *stenopetalum* (narrow-petaled).

YELLOW STONECROP,
Sedum lanceolatum,
Stonecrop Family, ¾ life size.

ALPINE AVENS,
Geum rossi,
Rose Family,
¾ life size.

ALPINE AVENS is the most common flower on the tundra. It grows in dense carpets, particularly in areas with relatively little snow accumulation in winter. Waving atop purplish-green stems, avens tend to be pollinated more by flies than by bees. Pollen-bearing and receiving flower parts (stamens and pistils) are well-exposed so that pollen transfers easily to and from a fly's body. However, fly-pollinated flowers, unlike those serviced by bees, tend to have little fragrance. In autumn, alpine avens foliage turns wide areas of tundra a lovely, deep red.

SNOW BUTTERCUP is the first flower to bloom on the tundra and in the upper subalpine zone. Frequently, it does not wait for snowbanks to melt, but bores a hole by the heat of its own respiration. Plants under 12 feet of snow have been found with half-open blooms.

Ranunculus means little frog and refers to the buttercup family's preference for damp places. Snow buttercups bloom all summer on the tundra, yellow swatches on otherwise dull brown ground in the wake of disappearing snow.

Snow buttercups really are cups, holding rainwater. The water floats pollen from the petals, where insects deposited it, to the stimga, where the yellow dust fertilizes potential seeds.

SNOW BUTTERCUP,
Ranunculus adoneus,
Buttercup Family, life size.

BUSHY or SHRUBBY CINQUEFOIL,
Potentilla fruticosa,
Rose Family,
¾ life size.

BUSHY or SHRUBBY CINQUEFOIL is common from the foothills to the tundra. Of the many cinquefoils, this is the only woody one, making it the easiest to indentify. *Fruticosa* means shrubby. Potentilla, which the many domestic varieties often are called, is Latin for little powerful one, a reference to the medicinal uses of some species. Cinquefoil (five leaf) comes from the French name applied to a European species that has five leaflets, radiating like fingers in a compound leaf.

GOLDEN BANNER or GOLDEN PEA is a very common flower that begins blooming in May on the plains and follows the summer up to treeline. Spreading by aggressive underground stems, golden banner can cover roadsides with masses of bright yellow. Pea-like pods that develop from the flowers are poisonous. Not eaten by livestock, masses of golden banner may be an indication of overgrazing. Botanists distinguish by seedpods three species that all wave under the same common name.

GOLDEN BANNER or GOLDEN PEA,
Thermopsis divaricarpa,
Pea Family, life size.

SULPHUR FLOWER,
Eriogonum umbellatum,
Buckwheat Family,
life size.

SULPHUR FLOWER is abundant in the sunny montane zone. Its flowers often turn rusty red in fall. Responding to soil and climate varieties, sulphur flower has adapted into many different species, including a diminuative alpine type *(Eriogonum flavum).* Sulphur flower honey is excellent, and livestock, particularly sheep, prefer this flower to other forage. Indians are reputed to have used sulphur flower in various brews to treat nearly any physical ailment, including hunger.

WESTERN YELLOW PAINTBRUSH is one of the few yellow Indian paintbrushes in the Rockies (see page 40). This yellow species of the subalpine zone and tundra frequently displays purple streaks from hybridizing with rosy paintbrush. A paler yellow paintbrush, northern paintbrush *(Castilleja sulphurea),* inhabits moist soils of the montane zone. Western yellow grows on unbranched stems, while northern paintbrush stems often branch.

WESTERN YELLOW PAINTBRUSH,
Castilleja occidentalis,
Figwort Family, ¾ life size.

YELLOW PONDLILY,
*Nuphar luteum
(N. polysepala),*
Waterlily Family,
1/10 life size.

YELLOW PONDLILY pushes up its large, shining leaves from a root embeded in the muck of shallow lake bottoms in the montane and subalpine zones. When leaves reach the surface, they uncurl to lie flat on the water, shading the pond and keeping the water cold. The flowers have their own strong stalks, extending from the mud. Besides providing cover for many pond animals, pondlilies supply ducks with seeds and muskrats with rootstalks to eat.

Indians also ate the large seeds, which taste something like popcorn. Squaws waded into the cold water to pull rootstalks from the mud. Indians also raided stores of rootstalks that muskrats had collected.

In Scandanavia, a troll called Näck sat at the bottom of lakes to fish for people to eat. His bait was the stem and flower of pondlily, called there the Näck rose.

YELLOW MONKEYFLOWER,
Mimulus guttatus,
Figwort Family, life size.

YELLOW MONKEYFLOWER and its pink and red relations inhabit wet areas. Their interesting shape reminds some folks of a monkey's face. Others fancy a resemblence to the tragic/comic masks of ancient Greek theater. *Mimulus* means mask. *Guttatus* means spotted and refers to the red spots on the yellow blossoms, part of the intricate pollination scheme that is the real reason for monkeyflower's unusual shape. The spots are nectar guides for directing insects to their food in the rear of the flower. When an insect goes for the bait, not only does it pick up pollen but also activates two lobes of the blossom to come together like a trap. Not tight enough to hold the insect, the trap is sufficiently tight to scrape off pollen the insect has carried on its body from another monkeyflower, insuring cross-fertilization.

CREEPING HOLLYGRAPE,
Mahonia repens,
Barberry Family,
¼ life size.

CREEPING HOLLYGRAPE is not a holly. Neither is it a grape. But it does creep along the forest floor, spreading by underground stems in well-drained soil, often that deposited by glaciers. The barbed, compound leaves are evergreen, although they often turn red in fall and winter. The yellow flowers form blue berries, which are favored by jelly makers, who race the birds, squirrels, and bears for them. Also called Oregon grape, a larger version grows in the Pacific Northwest. The similar Fremont mahonia lives with pinyons and junipers in the southern Rockies. Domestic mahonias are used widely for landscaping, especially to hold loose soil or rock on a steep slope.

MOUNTAIN GUMWEED is very common, especially on disturbed montane soil, during the heat of summer and through the first snows of fall. It is recognized easily by its round buds topped with beads of white, sticky goo. Perhaps because of its abundance, gumweed was used a great deal by Indians and the first Europeans in the Rockies in attempts to relieve the suffering of nearly all bodily ills. Indians even chewed it as chewing gum. However, because it absorbs selenium, gumweed is toxic if it grows in soil containing this poison.

MOUNTAIN GUMWEED,
Grindelia subalpina,
Composite Family, life size.

SMOOTH GOLDENROD,
Solidago missouriensis,
Composite Family, ½ life size.

SMOOTH GOLDENROD is one of nearly 100 species of goldenrod, difficult to distinguish from each other but widely-recognized as a group. The one pictured here waves its plume from the plains to the montane zone. Perhaps because goldenrod is so adaptable, widespread, and common, it has been used in an incredible variety of folk remedies and wild foods. Unjustly condemned by hayfever sufferers, goldenrod produces realtively heavy pollen that is spread by insects, not by wind. The only way goldenrod pollen can get into a human nose is on a bee's body, at which point hayfever becomes a minor worry. The flower's name perhaps comes from the use of some of the larger species as divining rods to find subterranean water or precious minerals.

GAILLARDIA, *Gaillardia aristata,*
Composite Family, ½ life size.

GAILLARDIA is one of the easiest composites to identify because its obvious red or reddish-brown center is unique. Another common name is brown-eyed susan. Ranging up to treeline, gaillardia is a mid-summer flower that tolerates heat and dryness. For this reason, varieties of it are cultivated all over the world. *Aristata* means bearded and refers to the hairy plant parts.

HEART-LEAF ARNICA is the easiest to identify of at least 14 species of arnica in the Rockies. Arnicas differ from many other yellow composites by bearing paired leaves opposite each other. Also, the petal-like rays of arnicas are the same color as the centers. Differentiating one arnica from another is considerably more difficult. However, heart-leaf is the only one with valentine-shaped leaves. It is common in moist subalpine woods. Since the Middle Ages, arnica has provided medicine to reduce swelling and infection. Arnica had an old name of leopard's bane, and Rocky Mountain campers who pitch their tents near arnica almost never are bothered by leopards.

HEART-LEAF ARNICA,
Arnica cordifolia,
Composite Family, ¾ life size.

LITTLE SUNFLOWER is yet another D. Y. C., "darned yellow composite." Yellow composites do a great deal to beautify the Rockies. They also do much to frustrate folks who want to identify wildflowers. Little sunflower and arnicas, for instance, look much alike. In composites, many individual flowers group together, simulating one flower head that does the work of many—efficient seed production through cooperation. Compound flowers are a relatively recent innovation in flower evolution. But the idea works well, and a great many species use it with rather slight, but maddeningly profuse, variations. At times, it seems as though all flowers are D. Y. C.'s, but these brash newcomers of all colors account for "only" twenty percent of the Rockies' species—so far. They mean to take over the world and probably will succeed.

LITTLE SUNFLOWER,
Helianthella,
Composite Family,
1/7 life size.

BLACK-EYED SUSAN,
Rudbeckia hirta,
Composite Family, ½ life size.

BLACK-EYED SUSAN grows abundantly on dry ground, especially along trails and roads. Its dark brown center, for which the flower is named, is cone-shaped and becomes ever more prominent as the seeds ripen. Its species name, *hirta,* means hairy, referring to the leaves and stems. The botanist Linnaeus, who started the system of modern scientific names, called this wide-ranging clan *Rudbeckia* to honor father and son Swedish botanists, both named Claus Rudbeck.

CUTLEAF CONEFLOWER,
Rudbeckia laciniata,
Composite Family, 1/20 life size.

CUTLEAF CONEFLOWER loves moist soil in the montane zone. Indians used a hot bath with a bushel of these plants to relieve rheumatism. They also used cutleaf coneflower to counteract the poison from snake or insect bites. Cheyennes boiled the leaves and stems, producing a yellow liquid that was believed to reduce poison ivy itch. However, cutleaf coneflower is somewhat poisonous to livestock, even to elk, deer, and bighorn sheep. Since these animals prefer to eat other plants, large patches of cutleaf coneflower may indicate overgrazing or soil disturbance.

ARROWLEAF RAGWORT, *Senecio triangularis,* Composite Family, 1/20 life size.

ARROWLEAF RAGWORT is abundant along subalpine streams. Three or more feet tall, it often hides the banks with its saw-edged triangular leaves. Toothed ragwort *(Senecio serra)* is similar but has narrow, tapered leaves. Ragworts also are called groundsels, a name derived from Anglo-Saxon words meaning ground swallower, for some species are very prolific weeds. *Senecio* comes from the Latin word for old man, and refers to white hairs on some species.

SALSIFY is very obvious after it has gone to seed (page 7). It looks like a tall, large dandelion and spreads with similar vigor. Less noticeable is the flower, which is distinguished easily by its green bracts, special leaves that extend conspicuously beyond the petal-like rays. Having immigrated from Europe, salsify has spread rapidly in waste areas and disturbed soils by virtue of its deep taproot and its winged seeds. *Tragopogan* is Greek for goatsbeard, another common name, referring to the white wings of the seeds.

SALSIFY, *Tragopogan dubius,* Composite Family, ¾ life size.

ALPINE SUNFLOWER or RYDBERGIA is the most conspicuous flower on the alpine tundra and one of the most interesting. (It is pictured on the next page.) Rydbergia blossoms are two to four inches in diameter and always face east. This adoration of the rising sun provides tundra travelers with a natural compass much more reliable than moss on tree trunks, particularly in an environment where trees cannot grow.

Probably alpine sunflowers produce such large blooms because they spend years developing a thick tap root and hairy, deeply-cleft leaves. After this preparation is complete, the plant bursts into its large blooms, luring many pollinating insects and setting many seeds. Then, the big show complete, Rydbergia dies.

Although very common every summer on the tundra, in some years waves of alpine sunflowers burst forth in awesome abundance. These wondrous displays are difficult to predict, but may occur in the summer after a particularly favorable summer for plant growth. The masses of yellow most likely will occur in soil disturbed by humans or gophers or in transition areas, where soil is gathering over rock.

Alpine sunflower also is called old-man-of-the-mountain because of its white, hairy coat that protects it from the cold and dehydration of brutal tundra climate.

WOOLLY ACTINEA is closely related to alpine sunflower, and the two plants are confused often. Woolly actinea has smaller flowers and usually grows very close to the ground. It sometimes is called stemless hymenoxys; a variety grows with a long stem in the foothills. Actinea grows among rocks in exposed positions, defying the wind with the protection of a woolly coat. Some contrary individuals of this very variable species lack the wool coat. Its leaves are entire, unlike Rydbergia's deeply indented leaves.

RED FLOWERS

MOSS CAMPION, *Silene acaulis* (Pink Family), invaded by **ALPLILY,** *Lloydia serotina* (Lily Family), and **ALPINE SUNFLOWER,** *Hymenoxys grandiflora* (Composite Family), ⅓ life size.

MOSS CAMPION or MOSS PINK is not a true moss, although its narrow leaves give it a mossy appearance. Its deep taproot enables this circumpolar tundra hero to pioneer in shifting gravel and sand. It grows relatively fast for a tundra plant: a cushion a half inch in diameter may be five years old; pink blossoms may appear at 10 and cover the plant by 20. In a quarter century, moss campion may be its maximum diameter of 7 to 12 inches. As it expands, moss pink captures bits of soil from the wind and hoards them under the cushion's many-branched stems. Eventually, grasses and other flowers, such as alpine sunflower, shown here, can invade this soil. In the course of centuries, cushion plants can be choked out as gravel and sand are converted to meadow.

QUEENS CROWN or ROSE CROWN,
Sedum rhodanthum,
Stonecrop Family, ½ life size.

Two sedums are very common on the alpine tundra. Queens crown and kings crown look rather similar and have the sedums' typical succulent adaptation to dry and otherwise inhospitable environments. Yet these two sedums are most common in sloppy marshes of the tundra and upper reaches of the subalpine zone. Ironically, these bogs are desert-like because the shallow-rooted sedums have trouble sucking water from the cold, acidic, compacted soils.

QUEENS CROWN or ROSE CROWN has a more spherical blossom than the typically flat-topped kings crown. Queens crown foliage turns red in autumn. *Rhodanthum* means rose-flowered. This photo of queens crown encased in icicles from the spray of a waterfall exemplifies the environmental trials suffered by all tundra plants.

KINGS CROWN is less limited to wet areas, venturing into rocky alpine soils. It is much darker, typically maroon, than queens crown. In late summer, the whole plant turns brilliant red, a spectacular contribution to the tundra's outstanding fall color display. Kings crown has a rose-like odor, which accounts for one of its common names, roseroot stonecrop, and for the *rosea* in its scientific name.

KINGS CROWN,
Sedum rosea,
Stonecrop Family,
½ life size.

FIREWEED is one of the first plants to come up after a forest fire or other disturbance. Spread efficiently by silky winged seeds, fireweed appears in magenta masses that hold the soil, provide valuable wildlife food and lift spirits knocked down by destruction. After the 1941 German air raids on London, fireweed invaded destroyed neighborhoods for the first time since Shakespeare. These weeds lifted the morale of beleaguered Londoners with an effectiveness that can be understood only by folks who have walked amid vibrant crowds of fireweed.

Botanists distinguish 100 species of fireweed wreathed around the northern hemisphere, 25 in the Rockies alone. Each of these bears its blooms on the end of a seedpod. *Epilobium* is Greek for "upon the pod." The most common species is *angustifolium*, which literally means narrow-leaved. From this characteristic, it also is called willowweed or great willow herb. For its sheer vibrancy, it has another common name, blooming sally.

FIREWEED, *Epilobium angustifolium*
Evening Primrose Family, ½ life size.

DWARF FIREWEED or ALPINE FIREWEED is but a few inches tall, dwarfed indeed compared to its three to five foot cousins. However, as is common among tundra species, its flowers are larger and brighter. Its leaves also are wider, hence the name *latifolium,* which means broad-leaved. Also found in the subalpine zone along streams, dwarf fireweed is most abundant in the northern Rockies.

DWARF FIREWEED or ALPINE FIREWEED,
Epilobium latifolium,
Evening Primrose Family,
⅓ life size.

LITTLE RED ELEPHANT,
Pedicularis groenlandica,
Figwort Family, life size.

LITTLE RED ELEPHANT herds are unlikely to trample hikers into the boggy earth. However, their spikes of pink flowers may lure their admirers to experience wet knees and elbows when getting down close to examine these delightful blossoms. Even the dullest eye can see the images of elephant heads. This fascinating shape is carefully adapted to facilitate pollination by bees. The flowerhead bends forward slightly with the weight of a landing bee. This causes the elephant trunk, which contains the potential seeds that need fertilizing, to gently whack the bee at the exact point between thorax and abdomen where pollen from another elephant likely is carried. The tight fitting ears and other flower parts force the bee to pickup more pollen as it enters for the nectar reward. The name *groenlandica* indicates the icy island where this flower first was found.

ALPINE PEDICULARIS,
Pedicularis sudetica,
Figwort Family, 3/5 life size.

ALPINE PEDICULARIS is a rare tundra flower also called Rocky Mountain lousewort. Pedicularis is a Latin synonym for lousewort, an Old English word reflecting a belief that livestock eating this flower (or a close European relative) became infected with lice. Wort stems from *wyrt,* Old English for plant. From Montana to Colorado, alpine pedicularis grows four to eight inches tall in damp tundra ground.

PARRY PRIMROSE is in the running for the title of most spectacular alpine and subalpine flower. Its intense magenta blossoms, which seem almost to glow from within, bloom 12 to 15 inches above bogs, streambanks, and other wet areas. They keep company with white marsh marigolds. Their red hue, like those of other plants, is due to one of the chemicals known as anthocyanins. Red color indicates anthocyanin contact with acid substances; blue betrays anthocyanin contact with alkalines. The odor of this flower is far less pleasant than its color, both of which serve to attract pollinating insects.

Charles Parry was a botanist in the West in the last half of the nineteenth century. His name is attached to many flower species.

PARRY PRIMROSE, *Primula parryi,* Primrose Family, ⅓ life size.

FAIRY PRIMROSE is an euphoniously named cousin of Parry primrose. With flowers that appear to be a diminuative version of its large relation, fairy primrose does smell much sweeter. This stricly alpine primrose grows only two to four inches tall, especially in rocky soil sheltered between boulders. One of the earliest tundra flowers to bloom, along with alpine forget-me-not, fairy primrose is a hint of the glory to come with Parry primrose in mid to late summer.

FAIRY PRIMROSE, *Primula angustifolia,* Primrose Family, life size.

**ALPINE CLOVER or
WHIPROOT CLOVER,**
Trifolium dasyphyllum,
Pea Family, and
ALPINE PHLOX,
Phlox condensata,
Phlox Family, life size.

Clovers are familiar flowers of the genus *Trifolium,* so called for their compound leaves with three leaflets. Typical of bee-pollinated flowers, clovers are very fragrant. Many small flowers usually crowd together in a dense cluster or spike, usually perceived as one clover flower atop the stem. Clovers are very nourishing for animals and also restore nitrogen to the soil. Of the 300 species, a few of the useful domestic clovers have gone wild in the Rockies. Three native clovers inhabit the alpine tundra.

ALPINE CLOVER or WHIPROOT CLOVER is a mat plant living in rocky terrain. Its showy two-toned flowers cluster in spheres that seem too large on a stem just one inch tall. *Dasyphyllum* means hairy-leaved, but the main leaf characterisitc is the sharp-pointed leaflets.

DWARF CLOVER is a less common mat plant whose flowers grow right on the ground. Each flower is relatively large, but since there are only two or three flowers per clump, the dwarves are inconspicuous compared to the many-flowered clumps of most clovers. *Nanum* means dwarf.

DWARF CLOVER,
Trifolium nanum,
Pea Family,
life size.

PARRY CLOVER is sweetly aromatic, lives in subalpine forests, as well as on the tundra and looks like clover that would grow in a lawn or beside a horse trail. It is named for Charles Parry, a pioneering botanist in the West whose name is attached to a great many different flowers.

PARRY CLOVER, *Trifolium parryi,*
Pea Family, ½ life size.

PYGMY BITTERROOT also is called least lewisia, a direct translation of its scientific name. Bitterroot, a near relative of this alpine and subalpine plant, is the state flower of Montana. Pygmy bitterroot ranges in color from pink to white. The lewisias are named for Meriwether Lewis, co-leader of the Lewis and Clark exploration. This expedition collected the first bitterroots seen by American botanists, who honored Lewis by naming the flower for him. Still a significant food for some Indians, bitterroot is said to sweeten with cooking, although Lewis did not seem to think so.

PYGMY BITTERROOT,
Lewisia pygmaea,
Purslane Family,
¾ life size.

WYOMING or NARROWLEAF PAINTBRUSH,
Castilleja linariaefolia,
Figwort Family, ½ life size.

SCARLET PAINTBRUSH,
Castilleja miniata,
Figwort Family, 3/5 life size.

Indian paintbrush is a multicolored group of some 200 species that tend to hybridize. Thus, while the group is easy to identify, individual species pose some problems. Paintbrushes tend to be parasitic, sending down some of their roots to penetrate roots of other plants to draw nourishment from the hosts. Thus, it is extremely difficult to grow paintbrushes in flower gardens. Seeds to be sown for landscaping around homes must be gathered from wild plants and bring well over $100 per pound. But it takes so many paintbrush seeds to weigh a pound that the labor must be done for love rather than money.

The flowers which produce the seeds are small and inconspicuous, hidden among brightly colored bracts (leaves) at the top of the stem. These bracts usually are mistaken for petals. A Spanish botanist discovered paintbrushes in Columbia and named them for another Spanish botanist, Domingo Castilleja.

WYOMING or NARROWLEAF PAINTBRUSH is very common in the sunny, open montane zone, especially with sagebrush, a favorite host. The state flower of Wyoming, this paintbrush usually has a green corolla (flower petals) protruding from the red bracts, just the reverse of the normal color scheme of petals and leaves. Wyoming paintbrush usually has several branching flowering stems. Its leaves tend to be very narrow, the meaning of *linariaefolia.*

SCARLET PAINTBRUSH inhabits moist ground in the subalpine and montane zones. Its form varies but it differs from Wyoming paintbrush by blooming on unbranched stems and lacking a conspicuous green corolla projecting from the red bracts. *Miniata* means red lead, referring to the scarlet color.

ROSY PAINTBRUSH exhibits a wide variety of colors, resulting from hybridization with yellow paintbrushes which share its subalpine and tundra environment. Frequently, rosy paintbrush is a key accent color in multi-hued floral displays that are among the main attractions of a wilderness mountain summer. *Rhexifolia* refers to the three prominent veins in rosy paintbrush leaves, similar to the pattern in a much less conspicuous group of herbs called *Rhexia,* including deer grass.

ROSY PAINTBRUSH, *Castilleja rhexifolia,* Figwort Family, ¼ life size.

BOG LAUREL or SWAMP LAUREL creeps across wet areas near treeline, often growing from a clump of moisture-holding moss. Non-woody parts of bog laurel contain andromedotoxin, poisonous to cattle, sheep, and humans. Even honey from its nectar may be toxic. Ten pollen-bearing stamens are held under tension in pleats in the petals. A visiting bee's weight springs the stamens loose to shower the insect with pollen, with which it fertilizes the next laurel flower it visits. Bog laurel leaves are evergreen and tend to curl under at the edges. *Kalmia* honors Pehr Kalm, who collected North American plants for the great Swedish plant namer, Carolus Linnaeus.

BOG LAUREL or SWAMP LAUREL, *Kalmia polifolia,* Heath Family, ½ life size.

GEYER ONION, *Allium geyeri,* Lily Family, ¼ life size.

GEYER ONION is easy to identify by the familiar pungent odor given off by bruised leaves or bulb. A similar relative is the nodding onion *(Allium cernuum),* which has pink, spherical blossoms that droop. Geyer flowers are upright. These wild onions are considerably more potent than the grocery store varieties. When General George Crook marched his soldiers beyond their food supply while chasing Sioux along the Yellowstone River, he was reduced to feeding his men on horse and mule flesh flavored with wild onion. Indians not only used onions for food, but also rubbed the whole plant all over their bodies to repel insects. Likely this technique repelled everything.

SHOOTING STAR, *Dodecatheon pulchellum,* Primrose Family, ¾ life size.

SHOOTING STAR is an aptly-named inhabitant of wet areas from the montane zone to the tundra. Masses of blossoms turn wet meadows pink in June. More than 15 species of shooting star range from Alaska to Georgia. They are closely related to the cyclamens of Eurasia, popular as domesticated house and rock garden plants in America. The pink darts of shooting star point in all directions from atop a leafless stem with a cluster of bright green leaves at its base.

PIPSISSEWA or PRINCE'S PINE is the most common pyrola in the Rockies. The pyrolas are evergreens with broad leaves and creeping underground rootstalks. Their stems are slightly woody at the base, and their blooms have a delicate, exotic appearance. They inhabit moist areas in the mountains. Pipsissewa is said to be a Cree Indian word meaning "it breaks into pieces." A brew from this plant was supposed to break up kidney or gall stones. Also called rheumatic weed, it was used by Indians to treat rheumatism. It sometimes seems as though nearly every flower was used against this ailment, which plagued people living the healthy life close to nature's winter snows and frigid streams. But pipsissewa actually may have helped. It does contain the same chemical used in aspirin today.

PIPSISSEWA or PRINCE'S PINE, *Chimaphila umbellata,* Heath Family, ¾ life size.

PINK SWAMP PYROLA or BOG PYROLA also is called shinleaf because a folk medicine use of the plant was to make plasters for injured shins. Pyrola comes from *pyras,* a word for pear tree, because pyrola leaves were seen as resembling pear leaves. *Asarifolia* refers to the resemblence of bog pyrola leaves to those of the *Asarum* genus, to which wild ginger belongs. Of course, all this concern with leaves clearly is beside the point to anyone gazing at the twelve-inch stalk of bright pink flowers gracing bogs and damp woods.

PINK SWAMP PYROLA or BOG PYROLA, *Pyrola asarifolia,* Heath Family, ¾ life size.

ROCKY MOUNTAIN RED COLUMBINE, *Aquilegia elegantula,* Buttercup Family, life size.

ROCKY MOUNTAIN RED COLUMBINE is a close cousin of Colorado's state flower (page 9), and the two can hybridize. Two similar red columbine species nod under the same common name in the montane and lower subalpine zones. Both prefer moist soil. Very similar red columbines are common in woods of eastern North America.

HORSEMINT or MINTLEAF BEEBALM, *Monarda fistulosa,* Mint Family, ½ life size.

HORSEMINT or MINTLEAF BEEBALM is typical of its family with a square stem and opposite leaves. Growing in clumps, it brightens roadsides, meadows, and gullies in the foothills and montane zone. It is a popular flower with bees and hummingbirds. Cattle sometimes will feed on it, but horses seem to avoid it, raising a question about the appropriateness of its name.

The scientific name, *Monarda,* is more logical. The Swedish botanist Linnaeus, who invented the double-name system of identifying species, named the flower to honor Sr. Monardez, a Spanish writer about medicinal plants. Domesticated in gardens, horsemint has been used for a wide variety of remedies and to flavor food. Actually helpful for some ailments, horsemint contains an antiseptic oil called thymol.

WILD ROSE by any other name would smell as sweet. Shakespeare's comment is comforting to folks trying to distinguish the at least 10 wild rose species in the Rockies. Nearly universal in distribution across America, the 100 species recognized by botanists hybridize so easily that mere mortals call them all simply wild rose. Wild prairie rose is North Dakota's state flower. From the flowers develop red fruits, rose hips, which are high in vitamin C and have all the delicious flavor of an old mealy apple with hairy seeds. They are valuable winter food for wildlife. From medicines, to teas, to perfume, the uses of this vigorous shrub are many and varied.

WILD ROSE, *Rosa woodsii,* Rose Family, ½ life size.

FREMONT GERANIUM is a common member of the famous family, of which there are several species in the Rockies. Most are similar to Fremont and are commonly lumped as wild pink geranium. The leaves turn brilliant scarlet in autumn. This plant honors John Charles Fremont, a controversial character in American history. He is remembered as a great explorer because he was considerably more literate than the rugged seekers of beaver pelts he hired to lead him through the West. Fremont was the first Republican presidential candidate, which usually is forgotten because Abraham Lincoln was the second.

FREMONT GERANIUM, *Geranium fremontii,* Geranium Family, life size.

BROWNIE LADY'S SLIPPER,
Cypripedium fasciculatum,
Orchid Family, ¾ life size.

FAIRY SLIPPER or CALYPSO,
Calypso bulbosa,
Orchid Family, ½ life size.

With some 35,000 species, the orchid family is the largest among flowering plants and contains many of the most spectacular blooms. About 25 orchid species grow in the Rockies, some even pioneering above the Arctic Circle, but the great majority are tropical. Their very specialized and complex pollination mechanisms, dependence on certain fungi, and narrow range of environmental requirements prevent most orchid species from surviving in large numbers. The orchid family may contain more endangered species than any other. Yellow lady's slipper, for instance, although slightly more adaptable than some other species, probably is the rarest, most endangered showy flower in the Rockies.

BROWNIE LADY'S SLIPPER also is very rare and endangered. Unlike most lady's slippers, this western flower has two to four blossoms in a cluster. *Fasciculatum* refers to this tendency. Brownie lady's slipper grows in shady subalpine forests, often in association with blueberries, heartleaf arnicas and Calypso orchids.

FAIRY SLIPPER or CALYPSO, named for the alluring nymph of Homer's *The Odyssey,* enchants wild lands around the northern hemisphere. Also called Venus' slipper, Calypso depends on decaying wood and on fungi involved in the decay process. Fairy slipper has to grow attached to fungi in order to absorb food and for its seeds to germinate.

One half of the double-sphered, bulb-like corm, for which Calypso is called *bulbosa,* produces a single glossy leaf in late summer. This distinctly veined leaf over winters, and from the other half of the bulb rises a flower stalk in spring or early summer. After a brief blooming, both flower and leaf wither.

SPOTTED CORALROOT is the most common and widespread of a group of saprophytic orchids represented by four species in the Rockies. *Corallorhiza* means coralroot and refers to the intricate underground stem, which really does resemble coral. It intertwines with dead plant material on which it feeds, having no chlorophyll to make its own food. Coralroots may be partially parasitic on pines, among which it lives in drier soil than most orchids tolerate. Spotlighted by a beam of sunshine in the summer woods, spotted coralroot appears in groups of reddish-brown, asparagus-like shoots. These leafless spears bear many attractive little blooms with spotted tongues. *Maculata* means spotted.

SPOTTED CORALROOT,
Corallorhiza maculata,
Orchid Family, life size.

TWINFLOWER is a dainty blossom named for a giant in the history of science. This was the favorite flower of the Swedish botanist, Carolus Linnaeus, who invented in 1737 the system of assigning a double name in Latin or Greek to distinguish species. The pair of delicately fragrant bell flowers rise on a single stem above evergreen leaves that form mats in shady coniferous forests. *Borealis* refers to the north; Linnaeus first saw twinflower in Lapland.

TWINFLOWER, *Linnaea borealis,*
Honeysuckle Family, life size.

SKYROCKET GILIA or FAIRY TRUMPET, *Ipomopsis aggregata,* Phlox Family, ¾ life size.

SKYROCKET GILIA or FAIRY TRUMPET attracts more than its share of hummingbirds. When they thrust their long bills in to get the nectar, their heads become coated with pollen, which the birds transfer to the next trumpet they visit. These showy flowers are biennials, establishing a rosette of leaves on the ground one year and sending up the flower the next. After it goes to seed, the plant usually dies, surrounded by the rosettes of its offspring. *Aggregata* means flocking together, describing the clumped colonies of skyrocket gilia. Other names are scarlet gilia and polecat plant, which refers to the skunk-like smell the upper leaves give off when crushed.

LAMBERT LOCO, *Oxytropis lambertii,* Pea Family, ½ life size.

LAMBERT LOCO is an extremely showy flower on sunny roadsides and meadows in the montane and subalpine zones. Very similar, but white in color, is Rocky Mountain loco *(Oxytropis sericea),* which tends to grow in clumps. When the two hybridize, the results are fields of multihued spectacle. The locos and some related milk vetches absorb high concentrations of some elements from the soil, barium in the case of Lambert loco, selenium in other flowers. Livestock usually avoid these plants unless overgrazing has eliminated good forage. But once they start on locoweed, animals become addicted, eat large quantities, and act crazy with various symptoms of poisoning. The tendency of certain plants to differentially absorb certain elements has been used in botanical prospecting to find uranium and to analyze the amount of heavy-metal pollution of land.

MOUNTAIN FIGWORT often is the commonest flower in shady subalpine forests. Its flowers' shape created the common names sickletop lousewort and parrotsbeak. Lousewort derives from the medieval notion that, when livestock ate plants of this family, they became infested with lice. Wort comes from the Old English word for plant. Stems and leaves of mountain figwort often are tinged with red.

WHITE FLOWERS

MOUNTAIN FIGWORT,
Pedicularis racemosa,
Figwort Family, ½ life size.

PEARLY EVERLASTING is very abundant with fireweed on burned over land or along roadside waste areas in the subalpine zone. Also called strawflower, this blossom can be dried for winter decoration without losing its form or color, a practice illegal on much public land where picking wildflowers is prohibited. *Margaritacea* means pearly. The stems usually are a foot tall. The narrow leaves are green on top but white with soft hairs underneath.

PEARLY EVERLASTING,
Anaphalis margaritacea,
Composite Family, ½ life size.

MARIPOSA LILY, *Calochortus gunnisonii*, Lily Family, ¾ life size.

MARIPOSA LILY is as widely praised as any flower can be. Its common name is Spanish for butterfly. *Calochortus* is Greek for beautiful herb. Utah designated the nearly identical sego lily as its state flower.

Utah honors the flower for saving Mormon pioneers from starvation in 1848. The whole plant is edible, but the gustatory prize is the bulb. Since these rarely exceed an inch in diameter and hide six inches underground, digging them up may reach a point of diminishing returns from the standpoint of relieving hunger. Besides, they are far too beautiful to destroy except in the most dire of emergencies.

Also called star tulip, these lilies often are pollinated by crawling insects. Since the insects eat the pollen instead of nectar, the flower must produce prodigious amounts of the yellow dust if any is to be left for fertilizing potential seeds.

DEATH CAMAS or WANDLILY, *Zygadenus elegans*, Lily Family, ½ life size.

DEATH CAMAS or WANDLILY bulbs sometimes were confused with mariposa lily bulbs by food-seeking Indians and whites. The results were disastrous. Livestock also is poisoned, by the stems and leaves. When death camas has bloomed, it is easy to distinguish from edible lilies, such as mariposas and onions. Various species of death camas, some deadlier than others, grow at all elevations. They pose no danger to those who wish only to partake of their elegant beauty.

SNOWLOVER, as its name implies, is a tundra flower that blooms in July and August where snowdrifts were deep in winter. *Chionophila* is composed of Greek words meaning snow lover. The flower first was discovered by Dr. Edwin James, who accompanied Stephen Long's 1820 military exploration of the West. James found snowlover on Pikes Peak, while in the process of becoming the first white man to climb a 14,000-foot mountain in North America. Behind him, James had left a smoldering campfire, which started the forest ablaze on the flank of Pikes Peak. All of James' supplies were burned, and he achieved a first of a less admirable sort.

SNOWLOVER,
Chionophila jamesii,
Figwort Family, life size.

BIG-ROOTED SPRINGBEAUTY is a tundra succulent whose rosettes spring from rocky crevices to defy alpine wind and cold. The rosette form, with very little vertical distance between leaves, balances the greatest exposure to light with the least exposure to cold, wind, and dehydration. It also creates the shortest possible distance from root to leaf. Radial symmetry also is efficient for dispersing water, food, and light, which come from all directions on the unshaded tundra. *Megarhiza* is Greek for big root—one to three inches in diameter—which this springbeauty sends down as far as six feet.

BIG-ROOTED SPRINGBEAUTY,
Claytonia megarhiza,
Purslane Family, ¼ life size.

WHITE MARSH MARIGOLD,
Caltha leptosepala,
Buttercup Family,
3/5 life size.

Three white buttercups grow in the same wet alpine and subalpine ground during mid summer. Often mistaken for each other, they really are not difficult to distinguish by folks who take a second, closer look.

WHITE MARSH MARIGOLD masses enliven areas recently freed of snow. Such extravaganzas should be photographed from a low height with a wide angle lens. Sometimes these flowers are so eager to blossom that they push their way up through unmelted snow. When melting snow finally does rush away, marsh marigolds hold their places with strong root systems. Their glossy, dark, heart-shaped leaves are thought to resemble bovine lips, resulting in the common names cowslip or elk's lip. *Leptosepala* means slender sepals, and refers to the radiant white, petal-like sepals, which sometimes have a touch of blue.

GLOBEFLOWER may grow adjacent to white marsh marigold. Globeflower sepals are broader and more cream-colored, a pale yellow when they first bloom. The most obvious difference is in the leaves, which have toothed edges, are divided into five lobes, and are much smaller than marsh marigold leaves. Globeflower got its name from a domestic variety, which has a more spherical flower than does the flat mountain species.

GLOBEFLOWER,
Trollius laxus,
Buttercup Family,
3/5 life size.

NARCISSUS ANEMONE or **ALPINE ANEMONE** gazes at its own beautiful reflection in tundra and subalpine marshes. Unlike the other two white buttercups here, it is hairy and bears three flowers on a stem. It usually is taller than the others and less likely to grow in masses.

NARCISSUS ANEMONE or ALPINE ANEMONE, *Anemone narcissiflora,* Buttercup Family, 3/5 life size.

ALPLILY (photos on pages 33 and 64) blooms relatively early on the tundra despite its scientific name, *serotina,* which means late-blooming. *Lloydia* honors a Welsh botanist, Edward Lloyd. Growing from a bulb the size of a green onion along an underground rootstalk, alplily may put up several blossoms in a line along the base of a rock. This flower is found at very high altitudes in remarkably separated locations around the northern hemisphere. Dainty, but tough, alplily grows between two and eight inches in height.

BLACK-HEADED DAISY is easy-to-identify among the 50-odd daisies in the Rockies because its involucre, the cup of bracts-leaves at the base of the flower cluster, is covered with black, woolly hairs. *Melanocephalus* means black-headed. Black-headed daisies grow in snow accumulation areas of the alpine and subalpine zones. When the snow finally melts in mid summer, the abundant sunshine and water enable these flowers to spring up and bloom quickly.

BLACK-HEADED DAISY, *Erigeron melanocephalus,* Composite Family, ½ life size.

BEDSTRAW, *Galium boreale,* Madder Family, ½ life size.

BEDSTRAW is everywhere abundant in the montane zone, but plants in moist areas bear more flowers in richer displays than those on sunny, dry slopes. Its seeds are ground as a substitute for coffee. Its service as a mattress filler gave bedstraw its name. Not only is it sweet smelling, but the hooked corners of its square stems and leaves catch on each other and prevent the bunches of bedstraw from matting down. The seeds also have hooks to catch on the fur of passing animals. This seed distribution system has spread the plant around the world in the northern hemisphere.

MOUNTAIN DRYAD, *Dryas octopetala,* Rose Family, life size.

MOUNTAIN DRYAD, a creeping shrub, forms mats on rocky tundra ground that is high in calcium. Its tough, evergreen leaves are important food for the ptarmigan, a rugged alpine grouse. Dryad also is very important in stabilizing slopes of loose gravel or scree. With its unyielding root system, dryad holds the rocks in place, traps organic material to form soil, and adds scarce nitrogen to the soil with nitrogen-fixing bacteria that live in nodes in its roots. After its flowers have matured to bunches of winged seeds, these downy clusters create another flower-like appearance before sailing away to colonize another scree slope.

WHITE BOG-ORCHID is common, though inconspicuous, in wet places in the subalpine zone. Since brightly colored little red elephants often grow along with it, the pure white spikes (one or two feet tall), of white bog-orchid are easy to overlook. Similar northern green bog-orchid *(Habenaria hyperborea)* and bracted bog-orchid *(Habenaria viridis)* also grow in such areas. White bog-orchid flowers merit close scrutiny, which permits enjoying the delicate aroma that earned this flower another common name, scent bottle. *Habenaria* is Latin for reins or narrow strap and refers to the narrow lip which some species of this large group exhibit. *Dilatata,* however, indicates that the lip of white bog-orchid is widened at the base.

WHITE BOG-ORCHID, *Habenaria dilatata,* Orchid Family, ½ life size.

SMALL-FLOWERED LUPINE fill sunny, dry areas in the montane zone and lodgepole pine forests in the subalpine zone. They house nitrogen-fixing bacteria in their roots, making the soil more fertile. In late summer and early fall, ripening lupine seeds produce alkaloids that can kill livestock, if the beasts gorge themselves on sufficient quantities. However, after the seeds are ripe, they seem to be safe and are consumed by elk and bears. Indians brewed a tea from ripe seeds. But for modern folks, who can select a wide variety of teas from the grocery, potentially poison lupine should not be consumed at all. *Parviflorus* means small-flowered.

SMALL-FLOWERED LUPINE,
Lupinus parviflorus,
Pea Family, 1/6 life size.

BROOKCRESS or BITTERCRESS,
Cardamine cordifolia,
Mustard Family, 1/6 life size.

SNOWBALL SAXIFRAGE,
Saxifraga rhomboidea,
Saxifrage Family, ¾ life size.

BROOKCRESS or BITTERCRESS blossoms abundantly along subalpine streams. It is a foot or more tall and has heart-shaped leaves, the meaning of *cordifolia.* Perhaps this physical coincidence accounts for the reputed value of brookcress in treating heart ailments.

SNOWBALL SAXIFRAGE blooms in spring in the foothills and montane zone. By summer it has appeared on the tundra and in the subalpine zone. On the tundra, snowball saxifrage usually is found in gopher gardens, soil disturbed by pocket gophers or meadow voles. *Rhomboidea* refers to the leaf shape which inspired another common name, diamondleaf saxifrage.

Saxifrage literally means rock breaker. The family is so named because some of these plants, which are rock garden favorites, grow in cracks in stones and tend to wedge the rock apart. Observing this process, makers of herbal medicines centuries ago assumed that the plants, when crushed, brewed, or otherwise ingested, would break up kidney stones.

The dubious medicinal merit of brookcress and saxifrage is based on the "doctrine of signatures." This old belief maintained that God created the various plants to serve human purposes and included in each plant's form or life cycle hints about how the plant could serve us. The shape of liverwort leaves, for instance, indicated that it should be used to heal the liver.

Such simplicity evokes smiles today. But how many folks still assume unconsciously that everything must be justified by its usefulness to mankind? Genesis 1:31 does not say, "God saw everything that he had made, and behold, it was very good for man." It does say that God declared everything good—period. To ask with arrogance instead of humility about anything in nature, "What good is it?" is ignorance just as deep as the doctrine of signatures. To assume that all nature revolves around mankind is idolatry as horrid as any condemned by the prophets.

But it is wrong also to view humans as totally divorced from the natural world, as complete aliens or infections that invariably sicken pristine natural systems. There is a disturbing modern tendency to define natural as a synonym of good and to define natural as "untouched or unaffected by human hands." Both these definitions of natural are far too narrow to accurately describe nature as it really works.

Like flowers, people are products of "the dust of the earth." Since we have a common origin, likely we will continue to discover quite unlikely ways in which plants and people do benefit each other. But such discoveries will be more complex than merely checking the shape of a plant's leaves.

STAR-FLOWERED PYROLA also is called woodnymph and shy maiden, names which indicate opposite types of personalities. Oddly enough, both names seem to fit this fragrant, waxy flower. Dwelling in cold, mossy forests, woodnymph loves subalpine stream banks. It is worth wet knees that result from kneeling to look up into her face. Of the nine pyrolas in the Rockies, this is the only one to have a single flower, hence its scientific name, *uniflora*. *Moneses* is derived from the Greek words that mean single delight.

STAR-FLOWERED PYROLA,
Moneses uniflora,
Heath Family, life size.

ARCTIC GENTIAN,
Gentiana algida,
Gentian Family,
¾ life size.

ARCTIC GENTIAN is the greenish-white trumpet that heralds the arrival of fall on the alpine tundra, where it is the last flower to bloom. Of the 1,100 gentian species that occur world wide, some 20 brighten the Rockies. Other prominent family members include fringed, star, and Parry gentians. Many gentians close their flowers except in bright sunlight. The family is named for Gentius, ancient king of the Adriatic country of Illyria, eventually conquered by Rome. This otherwise obscure king perpetuated his name by originating the legend that this prominent family of beautiful flowers had medicinal uses.

ALPINE PHLOX is a cushion plant pioneer of tundra gravels. Its deep taproot enables alpine phlox to hold its place in wind-scoured, shifting ground. Sometimes its white or faintly blue flowers cover the entire plant. Indians all over the West used various phlox species for ailments of the digestive system. Today, the chief phlox use is horticultural, for many domesticated varieties are very popular among gardeners.

ALPINE PHLOX,
Phlox condensata,
Phlox Family,
¾ life size.

YARROW is an abundant, long-blooming flower that is used to cure almost everything. In many cases, it actually works. Its scientific name comes from the Greek hero Achilles, who was said to have treated his soldier's wounds with a poultice from one of the 75 yarrow species that circle the northern hemisphere.

Yarrow sedates the nerves, soothes mucous membranes, and slows the flow of blood. It is an effective local anesthetic. Utes called yarrow wound medicine, and their white successors called it nosebleed plant.

Yarrow tea tastes just as bad as medicine is supposed to taste. When cattle eat yarrow, their milk tastes bad. Indian medical practitioners discouraged extended use, which could damage mucous membranes. Habitual use of any wild plant for medicinal purposes can cause dangerous side effects. But as a commonly available emergency pain-killer, yarrow can be handy.

Fern-like yarrow leaves inspired the name chipmunk-tail. *Lanulosa* means woolly, a reference to hairs on the stem.

YARROW, *Achillea lanulosa,*
Composite Family, life size.

RICHARDSON GERANIUM tends to be taller than the pink Fremont geranium (page 45). And the white species often blooms in pairs. Geranium comes from the Greek *geranos,* which means crane and refers to the long-beaked fruits produced by the flowers. Each geranium seed comes with a coil attached. When the seed falls to the ground, the coil twists and untwists with changes in humidity. If the coil rests against some stationary object, such as a grass blade, the coiling actions drill the seed into the earth, a self-planting mechanism. This geranium hybridizes with others.

RICHARDSON GERANIUM,
Geranium richardsonii,
Geranium Family, life size.

COW PARSNIP gains its scientific name from Hercules, an ancient hero who was said to have used it medicinally. Since this is a familiar story in which only the names change, it is easier to remember that Hercules was big and so is cow parsnip. Its umbrella-like flower clusters (umbels) can be a foot across. Common in wet areas in the montane and subalpine zones, it is eaten by wildlife as well as by cows. It can be consumed by humans and frequently was by Indians, although it tastes awful. The abundant hairs on the stems, for which the plant is called *lanatum* (woolly), will irritate skin around the mouth if they are not removed. Morever, extremely poisonous water hemlock could be mistaken for this semiedible cousin of the carrot.

Angelica *(Angelica ampla)* is another stout streamside parsnip with large umbels that often grows near cow parsnip. Angelica umbels are grouped in a spherical formation instead of the flat-topped form of cow parsnip. A much shorter version, *Angelica grayi,* grows amid rocks above treeline.

Water hemlock *(Cicuta douglasii)* can kill the person who mistakes it for an edible relative. A marble-sized chunk of root causes convulsions in humans. The treatment is to induce immediate vomiting. Livestock also are killed by eating water hemlock. The umbel-flowered killer is best identified by the leaves. They are compound, and the veins which lead to the edges of the leaflets end in the notches *between* the teeth. A better way to guard against hemlock poison is to stick to eating carrots or celery from the grocery or garden. This policy converts water hemlock to a delicate, attractive wildflower.

COW PARSNIP, *Heracleum lanatum,* Parsley Family, ½ life size.

PRICKLY POPPY,
Argemone polyanthemos,
Poppy Family,
⅓ life size.

PRICKLY POPPY is a plant of deserts, dry plains, and arid foothills that has immigrated into the mountains along barren road shoulders. As if the spines on this large beauty were not enough to discourage livestock from eating it, prickly poppy contains strong alkaloids that give it a bad taste. Since livestock avoid eating it, large numbers of this spiny flower can indicate overgrazing.

The poison seeds may contaminate food grains such as corn, oats, or wheat. Symptons of the poisoning are vomiting, diarrhea, blurred vision, swelling, coma, fainting, and general I-don't-feel-so-good. Doves, however, gorge on the seeds with seeming impunity. A relative of this flower was reputed to alleviate cataracts, hence the scientific name which comes from the Greek word *argema,* cataract of the eye.

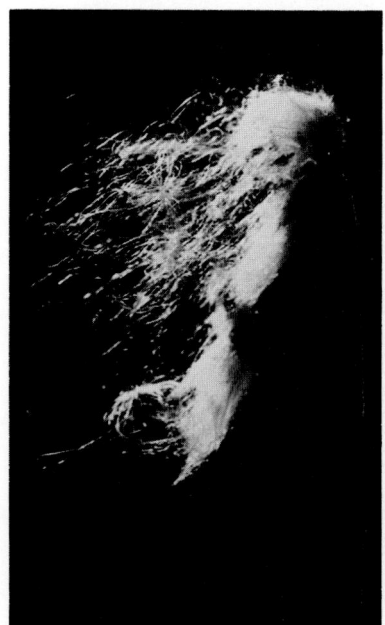

COTTONSEDGE is conspicuous in cold swamps and pond edges. It also is called hare's tail and cottongrass. Sedges differ from grasses in several ways, the most obvious to the touch being the sedge's unjointed, vaguely triangular stalk. Pollinated by the wind, cottonsedge also depends on wind to spread its seeds. The silky bristles that serve as sails for the seeds are modified petals and sepals of very small flowers. *Eriophorum* comes from the Greek words for wool bearing. *Angustifolium* means narrow-leaved. Of the several cottonsedge species in the Rockies, this is by far the most common, especially in the southern part of the range.

COTTONSEDGE,
Eriophorum angustifolium,
Sedge Family, life size.

MINERS CANDLE, *Cryptantha virgata,* glows in sunny montane fields in mid summer. Its hairy leaves and stem 10 to 24 inches tall overpower its small white flowers, and *Cryptantha* means hidden flower. The spike-like leaves with waxy white flowers at their bases are reminiscent of candle holders miners once stuck into mine walls to light their digging. Borage Family, ¾ life size.

INDEX

Achillea lanulosa, 59
Aconitum columbianum, 15
Aconitum napellus, 15
Actinea, Woolly, 32
Allium cernuum, 42
Allium geyeri, 42
Alplily, 33, 53, 64
Anaphalis margaritacea, 49
Anemone, Alpine, 53
Anemone narcissiflora, 53
Anemone, Narcissus, 53
Anemone patens, 14
Angelica, 60
Angelica ampla, 60
Angelica grayi, 60
Aquilegia caerulea, 9, 10, 44
Aquilegia elegantula, 44
Aquilegia saxhnontana, 10
Argemone polyanthemos, 62
Arnica cordifolia, 29
Arnica, Heart-leaf, 29, 46
Aster bigelovii, 11
Avens, Alpine, 23

Balsamroot, Arrowleaf, front cover
Balsamorhiza sagittata, front cover
Beargrass, front cover
Bedstraw, 54
Beebalm, Mintleaf, 44
Bistort, American, 5
Bittercress, 56
Bitterroot, Pygmy 39
Black-eyed Susan, 30
Blueberry, Dwarf, 19, 46
Blue Flag, Western, 14
Bog-orchid, Bracted, 55
   Northern Green, 55
   White, 55
Brookcress, 56
Butter-and-eggs, 21
Buttercup, Snow, 23

Cactus, Plains Prickly Pear, 21
Calochortus gunnisonii, 50
Caltha leptosepala, 37, 52
Calypso, 46
Calypso bulbosa, 46
Camas, Death, 50
Campanula rotundiflora, 18
Campanula uniflora, 18
Campion, Moss, 33
Cardamine cordifolia, 56
Castilleja linariaefolia, 40
Castilleja miniata, 40
Castilleja occidentalis, 25
Castilleja rhexifolia, 40
Castilleja sulphurea, 25
Chimaphila umbellata, 43
Chimingbells, Greenleaf, 16
   Tall, 16
Chinophila jamesii, 51
Cicuta douglasii, 60
Cinquefoil, Bushy, 24
   Shrubby, 24
Claytonia megarhiza, 51
Clover, Alpine, 38
   Dwarf, 38
   Parry, 38
   Whiproot, 38
Columbine, Colorado Blue, 9, 10, 44
   Dwarf Blue, 10
   Rocky Mountain Red, 44
Coneflower, Cutleaf, 30

Corallorhiza maculata, 47
Coralroot, Spotted, 47
Cottonsedge, 62
Cryptantha virgata, 62
Cypripedium fasciculatum, 46

Daisy, Aspen, 11
   Black-headed, 53
Delphinium barbeyi, 15
Dodecatheon pulchellum, 42
Dryad, Mountain, 54
Dryas octopetala, 54

Epilobium angustifolium, 35
Epilobium latifolium, 35
Eriogonum flavum, 25
Eriogonum umbellatum, 25
Erigeron melanocephalus, 53
Erigeron speciosus, 11
Eriophorum angustifolium, 62
Eritrichium aretioides, 16, 37
Erysimum asperum, 20
Erysimum navale, 20
Erythronium grandiflorum, 22

Fairy Slipper, 46
Fairy Trumpet, 48
Figwort, Mountain, 49
Fireweed, 35
   Alpine, 35
   Dwarf, 35
Flax, Lewis, 19
Forget-me-not, Alpine, 16, 37

Gaillardia, 28
Gaillardia aristata, 28
Galium boreale, 54
Gentian, Arctic, 58
Gentiana algida, 58
Geranium, Fremont, 45, 59
   Richardson, 59
Geranium fremontii, 45, 59
Geranium richardsonii, 59
Geum rosii, 23
Gilia, Skyrocket, 48
Glacier Lily, 22
Globeflower, 52
Golden Banner, 24
Golden Pea, 24
Goldenrod, Smooth, 28
Grindelia subalpina, 27
Gumweed, Mountain, 27

Habenaria dilatata, 55
Habenaria hyperborea, 55
Habenaria viridis, 55
Harebell, Alpine, 18
   Mountain, 18
Helianthella, 29
Hemlock, Water, 60
Heracleum lanatum, 60
Hollygrape, Creeping, 27
Horsemint, 44
Hymenoxys acaulis, 32
Hymenoxys grandiflora, 17, 32, 33

Ipomopsis aggregata, 48
Iris missouriensis, 14

Jacob's Ladder, Subalpine, 18

Kalmia polifolia, 41
Kings Crown, 34

ALPLILY
life size.